TOT
The Story of My Life

TOT
The Story of My Life

by
Bertha Lee Hughes Cruell

Published by Bertha Lee Hughes Cruell

ISBN 978-0-615-45083-4

Printed in the United States of America
TOT *The Story of My Life* by Bertha Lee Hughes Cruell

Dedication

This book is dedicated to my Lord and my Savior, the Man of men, and the King of kings. I am humble, grateful, and thankful for our Father, Lord God!

It is also dedicated to my wonderful grandchildren and great grandchildren, whom I love dearly, and to my Mother, who taught me independence and determination for rocky times. My mother is my angel who watches over me. Sometimes, before I open my eyes in the mornings, I can see Mama coming down in a cloud and touching my face, "My Angel!"

Acknowledgments

God - He is my true inspiration for this book.

Noah - My beloved, deceased husband. He always allowed me to grow.

Nell - She taught me that it is *okay* to move on and provided instructions on how to.

Joyce - She helped me to structure my life and spent countless hours, days, and weeks with me as I wrote this book.

Joy - She taught me to fear nothing and rise above weaknesses.

Maria - She allowed me to live my golden years with constant loving care.

Mary - She always supported whatever I attempted to do.

My grandchildren - They keep me young and in the kitchen.

My great-grandchildren - They all reflect family love and our family future!

Contents

1

The Reason I Write

I have always believed in the promises each new day provides, and that the best things in life will come to my family and me in the next season. My life has been filled with events, changes, challenges, blessings, and rewards. It has been my dream for many years to write about how I made it this far.

My writings began one morning at 3:00 a.m. in 1989. The room was dark. My husband and I were asleep. It was then a voice spoke to me. It said, "Get up. You are going to write a song." I sat up as the voice said, "I am going to give you the title of the song. The title of the song is 'My Man.'" I shook my husband and said, "Honey, wake up, listen to what just happened. God said something to me." My husband, who was half asleep, said "Yes, girl. Go back to sleep." I could not go back to sleep. I had never thought about writing, nor had I ever liked writing, but I was now being told that I would. After hearing God's voice, I was excited. I went to my bathroom and sat on the top of the commode as I wrote down what God said. I had to obey the spirit that spoke!

After that, I never stopped writing. I had life stories to tell. Ever since the Spirit spoke to me, I have written short stories. I don't know what it was, but I couldn't stop writing. I continued to write even after raising my oldest grandson, five daughters, as well as taking care of thirty beautiful nursery school children, for sixteen years. My writing continued as I served as the care giver for many sweet senior citizens, my sick husband, and my two elderly sisters. After my husband died, I was alone and had to make many difficult decisions. Even then, I still continued to write, because it was relaxing to me. I have great respect for writers. We could not do without them. They keep us informed with the world news, and they teach us how to be more successful in life.

After our family home was sold, I moved in with my second to youngest daughter, Maria, and her family. Besides going to church and meeting with some of the other senior citizens once a week, I have a lot of quiet time alone at home to write. I've enjoyed working on this autobiographical collection while everyone is at work and school.

This is my story!

2

A Sketch of My Early Life

I was born February 20, 1933 in North Mississippi. Everyone called me "Tot." I was the last of nine children born to colored sharecroppers in rural Madison County. My parents raised seven daughters and two sons as well as my oldest sister's daughter whom we called "O." My niece, O, was one year older than me, so we were like sisters. We lived in a handmade wooden house in Canton, Mississippi on a dusty road not far from Highway 51 near the cotton fields.

My childhood world revolved around what I called the "big house." The big house had a large center hall used as a family room with walls on each side that separated my parents' bedroom from the other bedrooms. On one side of the large hallway space were two bedrooms, one for the daughters and the other for the sons. My niece and I shared a bed and bedroom next to the front entrance door on one side of the center hall. There was a large fireplace in each of the bedrooms. The kitchen had a wood burning stove, a large table, chairs, and barrels to sit on and lots of pantry shelves.

We had no plumbing or running water in our house. A galvanized tub, which was kept on the back porch, was used for bathing and washing our clothes. Down the road, a little more than a mile, was the church, the schoolhouse, and the cemetery that were all on the same property. The schoolhouse had three classrooms used for primary grades, middle grades, and high school grades.

My father was a sharecropper, and my mother was our housekeeper as well as a cook for our landlord. I was a typical young child and teenager who looked forward to playing and meeting with my friends on Saturdays. In the late 1940s, when I was a teenager in Canton, Mississippi, the city was rife with racial injustice, inequalities, and segregation. Colored people were not allowed to have any of the rights, privileges, or opportunities that white people had. Colored children were never allowed to step inside the door of the same schools where the white children attended.

During that time Canton was a very small town that had no street bus service. There was only one police station, one court house, two colored funeral homes, two white funeral homes, two schools for coloreds, two schools for whites, one swimming pool, one post office, one colored day care center, several cafes, several colored beauty shops, several churches, one taxi cab, two barber shops, one train station, and one bus station where we often stopped to use the bathroom if we needed to. There were also two nightclubs, one of which was owned by my brother-in-law.

A couple of decades later Canton would become the focus of attention in a few films, highlighting the racial injustices. Changes slowly began to happen. In August 1994, Canton elected its first black woman mayor. The black woman candidate had received more votes. After the election, the white voters said they had found additional ballots that would have made the white candidate the winner. However, the local black lawyers filed a petition to block any more votes from being counted. The whites said, "Let's flip a coin, or let's have another election." After black people heard about what the white people wanted to do, black protestors began coming from all parts of the country. Everyone thought there was going to be a riot. The police and National Guard were there in the event that violence would occur. After years of racial segregation, injustice, and non-representation, the results were final; Canton now had its first black female mayor.

In September 1994 we saw another change come to our city. The movie *A Time to Kill*, based on the book of the same name, by John Grisham, was being cast and the setting was in Canton, Mississippi. The storylines were of a black man in Canton, or the fictional town of Clanton as told in the movie, fighting for justice for himself and his family after his daughter was attacked and raped by two white men whom he later killed, and the uprising of the Ku Klux Klan. These storylines, even told in a fictionalized book, showed to the world the horrid realities of racial injustice and violence towards blacks in Clanton and Canton, Mississippi. Another film *Waking in Mississippi: A Documentary on Race, Media and Politics in the Rural South*, was produced in 1997. This documentary actually highlighted the viewpoints of numerous local citizens of Canton regarding the racial injustices that black people in Canton had to endure. This all hit home for the town. Now, all we needed to do was clean up our hearts and put the hard times in the past.

Upon my several return trips to Canton as an adult, I had seen a big change take place in our city. There was a new fire department, a black chief of police, three super markets, a new hospital, one nursing home, three hotels, three jails houses, a county jail, and a dialysis clinic. There was a Popeye's Chicken and a Wendy's. Even though these new businesses had come to Canton, many people still drove to Jackson, Mississippi to work. There was also a Nissan plant which helped so many families by providing employment.

On one of my trips back I learned that my old church was rebuilt into a beautiful brick building at the city limit of Canton. My younger brother's funeral service was held at the new church. Every year Canton had a flea market fair in town. People from all over came to the fair by car, airplane, and train. There were many vendors spread throughout the city. Everyone walked freely and happily with ice cream or something cold to drink. There was so much shopping going on that people did not have any place to store all of the items they had purchased. Some people carried their shopping goods on bicycles or anyway they could get them home. After the movie *A Time to Kill* was filmed and shown to the world, things started to improve for Canton, particularly for the blacks who had endured racial injustices for so many years. Even though this was the only culture I knew, that colored people were treated differently than whites, still I didn't understand why.

3

Precious Memories of a Mississippi Childhood

I enjoyed listening to the rooster crow at the break of day. In my bedroom I had a mirror where I would watch the sun rise up behind the hills and trees; it was like a blaze of fire. I often took a yellow crayon and drew a happy face and smile in the mirror. It always made me watch the movement in the sky and how it changed. I never erased the beautiful sun in my mirror. It reminded me that every day is a happy day. When I looked in the mirror, it was always as if I could see right through me.

Birds and flowers always interested me. Bluebirds, robins, owls, and crows could always be seen near the big house. I enjoyed lying on the porch watching and wondering what made them able to fly and grow.

We lived close to the road, and there were other sharecropping families living near us. However, some families who lived about a half mile down the road had to walk past my house to get to the church and school. Only a few people in our area had cars back then.

On Fridays, after chores, our friends would come to visit. We played games such as "catch me if you can" and "Mary Mac." We also jumped rope, using a rope made from twine we found around the house, and we always sang songs.

My favorite childhood memory was the playhouse that I made under the big house. I had to get on my knees to walk around under the big house, but I really enjoyed my playhouse. One of my big sisters let me have a mirror that I hung as decoration. Old newspapers and magazine pages were used to cover the walls as a sort of wallpaper in our big house, and I also used them to cover the walls in my playhouse. It was also my secret hiding place from Mama during the day, if I misbehaved and needed a spanking.

I also had dolls for my playhouse. Mama made me a handmade rag doll, and I made my own dolls by using curvy Coca Cola bottles. The glass bottle was used as the doll's body, and the silk from fresh corn ears was used for the doll's hair which was held in place by wooden clothes pins that were stuck into the top of the bottle. I used old pieces of fabric, leaves, and other things to make clothes for my dolls. I used clay bricks for a doll bed, dresser, and other furniture.

Duke, our family dog, and I had the run of the house. Sometime Duke and I sat on the porch at night watching the moon, cloud, and the stars. I talked to him when the clouds formed different symbols. I'd say, "Duke, did you see that? It's shaped like you."

Sometimes it was the shape of a person, an animal, or other symbols. Duke was a mixed breed, but he was a sweet, big, brown and white dog. I grew up with him, and he took care of everyone. When Duke died, my younger brother took a shoebox and dug a hole for the box, but the box was not big enough to hold Duke. He then built a wooden box for the hole, and we put Duke in the grave. We copied a program from the church and picked some beautiful flowers from Mama's garden for Duke's private funeral. We dropped a flower on top of the box. We prayed, cried, and hugged each other. Then, my brother covered the grave, and Duke was gone.

4

Mama

Mama, with her smooth black skin, high cheekbones, and long coarse black hair that was always kept in a tight bun on her neck, was my angel. She named me Bertha, which was also her name. Mama was a quiet and very spiritual woman who worked from the time she got up in the morning until after I went to bed at night. Her father was George Lewis, and her brother, my uncle, was named David Lewis. At that time birth records were kept in family Bibles. The most reliable record of births was usually what elderly family members told you. However, throughout the years, many family members were split-up for various reasons and moved out of the area, which made it difficult to maintain reliable records.

Mama raised chickens, ducks, pigs, and turkeys that sometimes ran away. She also had a vegetable garden on the side of our house. Mama had my father dig a small pond in the backyard just for the ducks. She often shared vegetables from her garden with the neighbors. During the fall season, women from the neighboring houses came over to make beautiful quilts. They usually spread the quilt out over several chair backs as they sewed it together. I loved laying under the quilts and listening to the women sing and talk as the flames in the fireplace hypnotized me into a calm sleep. Oftentimes, they woke me so that I could help them thread their needles. This was a job I felt was very important, because it gave me a special part in helping to finish the beautiful quilts.

In the front of our house was Mama's beautiful flower garden which could be seen from the highway. People often stopped by and asked to buy some of her flowers and vegetables. In the vegetable garden, Mama grew mustard greens, collards, cabbage, beans, peas, squash, carrots, potatoes, and corn. In her flower garden there were many different kinds of flowers, most of which she grew from seeds. Sometimes she also dug wild flowers from the woods and replanted them in her flower garden. The multiple colors of the flowers were breathtaking. Mama definitely had a "green thumb," because she could grow anything.

Fishing was Mama's favorite thing to do to relax, and she enjoyed going fishing alone. She said that she could think and pray better. Duke always accompanied Mama on her fishing trips. He was the reason that we never had to worry about her when she went fishing. Duke sat there quietly while she fished.

When Mama got ready to move on to another fishing spot, Duke would also move, until they were ready to go home. Upon her return from the fishing creek, we looked forward to eating perch, catfish and sometimes turtle for our supper.

The white landlord whom we called "Boss" lived across Highway 51 with his family. His house was within seeing distance from the front porch of our house. Boss was also our mailman, and he had a daughter my age. The landlord depended on Mama to be his family's cook. Mama ate the same food that she prepared for them, and on many occasions she brought home the leftovers for our supper. Rather than work in the cotton fields, I was needed around the house to help Mama. I learned that working in the hot heat of the cotton fields made my skin bake, and that was not good for me. Life, as I remember it, was not easy but full of faith and love for family.

Even though coloreds and whites didn't mingle, I was allowed to play with the boss's daughter. I was made the water girl for the families working in the fields, and I also took water into the house. One day the boss said to Mama, "On some days, you bring your girl to play with my girl." I remember playing with his daughter when I was a small child while Mama worked there, but that white man never let my niece O, whom I loved like a sister, go over to play at his house. I never understood why that white girl and I played together. We played with each other until I was about eleven years old, and then I never saw her again. I was never told why. It was later in my adult life that I realized that my niece's skin color was lighter than mine and may have contributed to the boss's attitude and behavior.

5

Papa

Willie Hughes was my father. His nickname was "Bip." He loved his baby girl Bertha whom he nicknamed "Tot," because I was so small. I called my father "Papa," and he was my hero. When I looked in books and saw Indians, I thought Papa was an Indian. His skin color was a beautiful reddish-brown, and his hair was coarse and straight at the same time.

I believed my father could do anything. He was a wise man who was creative with ideas. To keep us from hauling water from far away places, Papa drilled for water on the side of our house. He dug, and dug until he struck water. After he struck water, he set up a pump at the drilling site to make it easier for us to get the water from underground.

Papa's creativity and hard work were also noticed by the boss. He built houses for other sharecroppers on the property as well as slaughtered hogs and picked cotton in the fields. Papa had to fill long sacks with cotton that weighed over 400 pounds, and then he had to pull the sacks through the fields to the scales for weighing. Sometimes Papa let me ride on top of the sacks when he took the cotton to the scales. The sacks moved up and down through the bumpy fields, and I enjoyed the ride. It was so much fun! After weighing each sack, Papa would return to the fields to fill the sack again.

Sometimes during my visits to the fields, I walked behind Papa telling him about my hopes and dreams. He was a good listener, and he said that I was a comfort to him by being there. I told him that someday I wanted my own house that did not have a landlord or chickens in the yard. I remember asking him to build us a brick house where we lived. He said, "Tot, I can't build you a brick house." One day Papa put brick-like panel boards on the front of our house. Our house was no longer a grayed out weatherboard looking house, but now a yellow and brown beautiful brick looking house on the front. I loved looking at it when coming down the dusty road.

Papa was also the landlord's handyman. Whatever the boss wanted him to do, Papa could do it, even when he had to pick a lot of cotton. I never understood why Mama, who cooked the boss's meals, and I were allowed to eat in his kitchen with his daughter, but my father did not come in the house. Papa ate his meals while sitting on the back steps. One day I asked Papa why he never ate in the kitchen with us. He responded, "Baby, I'm too sweaty and dirty." I later learned that he couldn't come into the kitchen because he was the boss's handyman and not allowed to eat at the boss's table.

Papa was fearless; however, the only thing that I knew he was afraid of was a storm. If a storm were due, wherever Papa was located, he returned home before dark. Sometimes before bedtime, he would say, "A storm is coming tonight." He always sat and listened to see if the wind got stronger. He then went outside to see which way it was coming from. After he determined the direction of the wind, he would tell us that a storm would hit about midnight, and that it was coming our way. He told us to get up from bed and put our clothes on. I remember asking him why we needed to put our clothes on. His answer was, "If for some reason, God forbid, things happened or changed, everybody would be fully clothed." He wanted us to be prepared if we needed to escape the house from the storm.

I have several fond memories of Papa from my childhood. A memory that stands out to me the most was when I was about thirteen-years-old. Papa took my niece and me to his baseball games every Saturday. He and the other men were all very good players, and Papa was the umpire. The players were always very glad to see Papa, because he usually took and shared the white lightening liquor that he and his friends had made in the woods.

6

Siblings

Even though I couldn't play with the boss's daughter anymore, I still had my nieces and nephews to play with. Most of my sisters, who were so much older than me, had left home, except for two. Some lived in other cities or in town. At the age of thirteen or fourteen, O moved to live with one of my big sisters. After she left, I missed her terribly, but we always kept in touch.

When the crops were slow, Papa stayed with my sister in New Orleans where he worked on the riverfront hauling cargo. This job paid good money, and it helped to replace the money he could not make in the fields. While Papa was working in New Orleans, Mama, my brothers, and I stayed home to take care of the house, animals, and the crops. He often used some of his salary to purchase things to make me happy. On one occasion I told Papa that I wanted a bicycle, and he brought back a beautiful blue bicycle for his Tot. I was the only child in our family and the neighboring houses with a bicycle.

My brother David Lee, who was called "Pete," was very much like Papa. He was good with his hands and learned to make caskets. Pete moved to New York to live with my sister Mattie Bell and her husband. There he also learned the barber trade and was considered one of the best in his barber shop. After he moved to New York, I did not see Pete again until thirty years later when we were both adults. It was a blessing to see him again, because I thought he would never return to the South.

My older brother was Wilbert, who we called "Bam." Bam thought he was God's gift to women, even though he was crossed-eyed. The city doctors said that his eyes could be fixed, but Mama and Papa did not have extra money for Bam to move to the city and to have an operation. Bam did not want the operation anyway. He said he could see just fine. Everyone in town knew Bam. He was the local handyman, and he also helped out in a family cafe. Bam called himself "player-player." The colored and white people thought he was one of the most liked colored men in Canton. The white folks often provided him with food, clothing, and a place to stay. They knew he was an honest man willing to earn his keep after leaving his family home. Upon his death, many years later, his funeral was attended by many of his family, friends, and numerous white people. When I look back at Bam's celebration of life, I am grateful that my children and husband were present to witness his homegoing.

My big sisters were like extensions of my mother. Mama, who was quiet and homely, let them take charge of me. They loved me, and I loved them dearly. This also meant that they checked my schoolwork and disciplined my behavior.

My sister, Geneva, and her husband had four children. My niece and I were their babysitters. Whenever Geneva needed us to babysit, Mama made us walk the mile or more trip to Geneva's house. I remember one day we had to watch the kids, and I said, "No." My sister replied, "You said, 'no?' Mother sent you both to help me. Are you disrespecting me and Mama?" I was so mad, because I wanted to go out to play. I will never forget what happened when Geneva and her family came over to our house on the following Sunday. Being "Miss Big Person," I spat on the ground near Geneva when she and her family arrived in the yard. Geneva surprised me, and grabbed my little body and swept my mother's yard with me. I never disrespected my sister again. Mama ran to the yard and asked, "What happened?" When Geneva told her, Mama said, "Geneva, you were right. This family takes care of one another. That is my demand."

During my youth, Geneva's husband was one of the meanest men I had ever known. He was violent and abusive to my sister. Because I was their babysitter, I was always around them and got to see the abuse regularly. After seeing how abusive Geneva's husband was to her, I learned that I didn't want anybody, especially my husband, to beat me. Spousal abuse was very common in the rural areas, particularly on weekends when there was more time to drink liquor.

My sister Willie Mae, whom I called Bill was called "TeeTee" by her nieces and nephews. She never had any children of her own, but she helped all her nieces and nephews in many ways. She always showered family members with gifts of money and clothes which she sent through the mail. I believed in God, Santa Claus, and "Tee-Tee." Tee-Tee married a white man named Jim, and they both lived in Reno, Nevada. For many years she showered us with Christmas gifts, money and presents. We kept in touch with Tee-Tee all of her life.

Tee-Tee and Jim were not our only family in Reno. Some of my cousins also lived there. Tee-Tee and Jim came to visit New Orleans several times. She retired from Harold's Casino in Reno where she was a hat and coat check girl for many years.

My big sister Mattie Bell was the last one to move away from home. She used to comb my hair, talk to me about the future, and hug me all the time. When Mattie Bell got married I felt like someone had died. After her wedding she and her husband moved to town. My older sister Sally was the free spirit according to Mama. There wasn't anything she was afraid of.

My sister Lula, whose husband was a minister, took care of Mama during her illness. Sally and Lula took turns caring for Mama. Mama died in Sally's arms. My sister Thelma, who was O's mother, was deceased at the time of Mama's death.

On numerous occasions my siblings, as well as my niece O, would returned home to Mama and Papa. If things were not going well in their relationships, they would return home to Mama and Papa to get away from their spouses. I was always happy to have them back home. We would sit on the porch at night with the lightening bugs flying about, the full moon out, the smell of honeysuckle in the air and the wind blowing, talking and enjoying each other. Some nights we could hear the sounds from the church down the road. It was all very comforting.

7

Faith

Growing up in our house was like most households in our rural community. We got up when or just before the rooster crowed. Mama taught me to thank the Lord before I started my day. Most children did chores before walking the mile or more to school, unless they skipped school to help out in the cotton fields.

There was a Methodist minister who preached at the church down the road where my family worshipped. Even though it was a Methodist church, there were Baptist people who attended too. As a child, I did not know the difference between the two denominations. All I knew was that we listened to the preached word, sang gospel songs, prayed, clapped our hands, and treated each other with respect and family like love. The older people pinched us kids and put fingers to their lips if we tried to talk to our friends during the church service. We also had to wear something white on our head to take communion. This was a very special Sunday, and we tried extra hard to be humble and good before and after the service.

Mama and Papa could not read well, but my sisters and a brother could. They read the Bible to Mama and Papa, and Mama told us how Jesus wanted us to act. I enjoyed listening to Mama sing old hymns throughout the house while cooking or doing chores.

Being around praying folk and church always left me with a good feeling and love for Jesus. After some conversations, confessions, and much prayer, I went up to the front of the church and told them that, "I accept Jesus as my Savior. I believe He was the son of God. I also believe that He was sent to teach us how to live, and that He rose from the dead." My baptism was in a pond with other new believers. We all had on white clothing that the church folk had given us to wear in the baptismal water. I was baptized in 1947 as Methodist, but in my adult life I became a Baptist.

8

Rollercoaster Ride

Children were not allowed to be present when grown folks were having adult conversations. So, I did not understand things about segregation and integration when these were the topics the adults were discussing. I did recognize that colored people were not treated the same as white people. In town, I knew that colored folks could not eat at some cafes unless they were passing for white people. Colored people could not do the same things that white people could. I didn't understand why, but I knew this was not right. I asked Mama about this, and she said, "God will change things, but you just do as you are told."

I remember one night, it must have been after midnight, when a knock on the door woke my niece and me. Our bedroom was on the right side of the front door. Papa and Mama slept in a room on the other side of the center hallway. I heard Papa open the door. I could hear several grown folks talking, and I recognized that my uncle and his mama and daddy were talking.

My niece and I put our ears to the wall, but we could not understand what they were talking about. All I felt was that somebody was in a lot of trouble.

When the grown folks stopped talking, my niece and I jumped back into the bed. Later, someone knocked on our bedroom door and slowly came into our room. It was my father and my uncle along with his mama and daddy. Papa said, "Girls we need you to get dressed and go with your uncle and his mama and daddy for a ride in the truck." We were confused since it was so late, and we were usually asleep at this time. Mama said "Girls, it's okay–put your clothes on." My uncle's mama said, "Darlings, put your sweaters on, you will be riding in the truck, and it might get cold on the long ride."

My niece and I got in the back bed of the truck, and they covered us both with some kind of heavy material or canvas. My uncle told us that we would be fine and not to worry. They drove us for what seemed like a long time down dusty roads and along the train tracks, and then we crossed over the train tracks and into the woods. They told us to get out of the truck, and they put the truck in some thick bushes. Then they put tree limbs and bushes over the truck to cover it up and hide it.

It was dark, but my uncle had a light on the hat that he wore. He had a long knife that he used to cut a path for us to walk on a trail through the woods. I told him that I was scared, and his daddy told me and my niece that we would be fine. We were told to keep close together while we walked through the woods, guided only by the light on my uncle's hat. He told us that we had to get to a highway. After we reached the highway, the light had to be turned off. My niece and I clung close together like we were told. There was another truck waiting across the highway in some bushes. We got in the truck and were covered up like before. We rode again until it was almost morning. I heard that we had gone to the Mississippi Delta where my uncle's brother and sister-in-law lived. That is where we spent the day.

When we got to a house I learned that it was the house where my uncle's brother and his wife lived. My uncle and his mama and daddy got out of the truck and said, "We're here!" A lady came out of the house and said, "He's in the fields. Let me get him." The person she called was my uncle's brother. His family had not seen or heard from him for a long time.

We spent the whole day at that house. There was a big meal prepared for the occasion. I can still taste the banana pudding we had for dessert. The pudding was so good that my niece and I thought the delicious taste of the dessert was worth the scary truck ride and walk through the woods.

After the visit to the Delta, we started back home after dark. We went back the same way we had gotten there. On the highway we followed the trail and found the hidden truck. We got in and rode back to Madison County.

I learned later that the uncle we had gone to visit had relocated to the Delta, because he had been accused of beating up a white man. He would have been killed if he ever set foot in our county again. My niece and I were taken along on the ride just in case the police or bad people saw or stopped the truck. If the trunk had been stopped, the children riding along would have kept the police or bad people from thinking something was wrong. I will never forget that day.

9

Hard Decisions

When I was a teenager, O, my niece, moved back into our house with Mama, Papa, my big sister, and me. Now that we were older and our personalities were different, my niece and I had our own separate friends from school. When I was in junior high school I was very popular. I was in the Four H club, and we wore red, white, and blue uniforms. On the Fourth of July, we walked in a parade around our town holding the American flag. On some days our teacher took us on field trips in the woods, hiking, or just looking for anything interesting. There were many trees in the woods including cedar and oak trees. We looked for trees with nuts, moss, bark, and sometimes berries. After returning from our field trip, our teacher made space to display our exhibits that we found in the woods or on our hike.

The young people enjoyed getting together on the weekends at the local café in the county. Our uncle was the owner of this café, and I often saw him there when I went with my friends. This is where I began dating. Even though I was told to keep my dress down, I became pregnant at fifteen years old shortly after I started dating my first boyfriend.

Ms. Bird, who was my principal and teacher in high school, was the first person with whom I shared this information, and I had not yet shared it with my mother or my sisters. I was so afraid to tell her. I cried to Ms. Bird, and she held me close in her arms and helped me. She said, "Honey what is wrong with you?" I said, "I am so afraid to tell my family, I don't know what to do. I am pregnant, and I may never graduate from high school." She said, "Oh yes, you are going to graduate." I said, "How?" She said, "You are too smart to let go. You will be the first one, but you will be able to graduate." She went to visit and talk to my mother. My mother was sick at the time, and I did not know if she would be able to bear hearing the news that Ms. Bird was going to tell her. Ms. Bird said, "Even though you are in the tenth grade you are so close to graduating, and you will be promoted to the eleventh grade." In spite of what Ms. Bird was telling me, I decided to stay home to take care of my mother.

The father of my baby was twenty-years-old at the time, and I was fifteen. Mama had told me about how babies were made, but I did not understand how my inner feelings could affect my decisions once I began dating. My daughter's father had moved to another state months before I found out I was pregnant. He heard about my pregnancy from his family in Canton, and he came back to do the honorable thing with the intention of marrying me.

He asked my parents for permission to marry me. He was sincere and had good intentions. He knew that I was young and innocent. I remember that he was smart and that he was a good man, but I did not love him and did not want to marry him.

My sisters, Bill and Sally, argued with him something awful. Bill said, ''Tot, you don't have to marry him if you don't want to. I will help you with the baby." My father said, "Tot, what do you want to do?" This was a very difficult adult decision I was faced with. I knew that my life was about to change forever. I said "no" to marriage.

Just in case I changed my mind, my daughter's father stayed in town until after she was born. He went back to his new home out of state when she was a few months old. I never saw him again. I dropped out of school and prepared to live with my decision through the grace of God. I named my new baby "Nell."

10

Motherhood

The hospital was in town, and we lived in the rural county. Doctors only came to the rural areas for emergencies. The local midwife had come to visit me a few times during my pregnancy and told me all the dos and don'ts.

The evening of November 9, 1948 I went into labor. Mama, Papa, my big sister, and the midwife were with me at home. Papa had walked over a mile to get the midwife for me. I will never forget how horrible the labor pains were. My sister said that going through labor pains and having a baby were going to make me a woman.

My baby girl was beautiful with a head full of hair. I counted her fingers and toes, and kissed her all day and night. I told her that I would take good care of her. Nell was a good baby and was loved by my family.

After the delivery Mama bound my stomach with broadcloth and pulled it tight the way the midwife told her to. I was not allowed out of the house for two months. My family helped me at home with my baby, because Mama was still cooking for the landlord. I had to learn new things very quickly and had to learn to make adult decisions. Even though I had a baby, I still wanted to go back to school.

One of my sisters, who lived in New Orleans, said there were jobs there. She also said that I could come to New Orleans to get a job, or I could go to school to train for a good job. She asked if I wanted to live with her until I could get on my feet. I took her up on her gracious offer.

My parents and sisters in Canton agreed to help keep my daughter while I worked in New Orleans for a while. My sister in New Orleans mailed me a train ticket and instructions for my trip. She had a good friend who was a porter on the train, and he was supposed to look after me. Mama packed me a lunch, and I packed one suitcase. I held my one year old daughter and kissed her and told her that I would be back as soon as I got a job and could take better care of her.

11

Moving Onward

New Orleans was everything I was told it would be and even more exciting than I thought. At that time there were all sorts of jobs available. There were cars driving everywhere. Many colored ladies in uniforms walked the streets going to work. There were jobs in sewing factories, bakeries, hotels, and dry goods stores run by Jewish people who treated colored people fairly. I learned about the public trade school and wanted to attend, but I knew I had to get a job first.

My sister took me to find a job, and I was hired after two weeks of searching. I worked in a hotel dining room folding napkins and helping out. The supervisor, who was also the secretary, took a liking to me, and I told her I was the mother of a one year old. She said, "You're just a baby yourself." My supervisor fixed my schedule so that I could visit my baby and family at least once a month and sometimes twice a month.

I sent most of the money I earned home by mail, because I didn't have to pay for rent. My sister would not accept money from me, because she wanted to help me save. Our family had a belief that family took care of family.

After a few months I started working at a company that manufactured lingerie and underwear. My job was to place four items to a box for shipping. The pay was more than what I made at the hotel dining room job.

Tot as a Young Lady

When my sister moved back to Mississippi, I moved in with another sister and her husband, who also lived in New Orleans. They did not have children. They were very nice to me. Because I was a friendly young lady, it was easy for me to make friends at work and in my neighborhood. I wrote home to Canton telling everyone about the children who lived in the house next door to me, and how we played jacks with small rocks and a ball, kick the can, hide and seek, hop scotch and jumped rope. Even though I was sixteen and a mother myself, I looked forward to this playtime after work and chores.

12

The Love of My Life

One day, while boxing lingerie at work, my co-worker friend said she wanted me to meet a young man whom she knew. She added that it was time I stopped playing with children, and she also said I would probably like this young man for company or dating. She described him and said he was my age and that he was also from Mississippi. Our plan was to go to the local lounge on the weekend to dance and have fun. I looked forward to our night out.

After we arrived at the lounge, my co-worker's boyfriend walked over to our table with a big, handsome young man. The young man seemed somewhat shy. He was introduced as Noah and sat next to me. We talked and danced all evening. I quickly realized that I liked this strong young man, because we were able to talk easily. I gave him my phone number and address, and he wrote it down on a napkin and put it in his pocket.

Noah showed me how a gentleman was supposed to act and how a young lady was supposed to be treated. He held my hand so gently when we danced, and slid the chair out from the table so that I could sit down. He also paid for the drinks and snacks I ordered. My girlfriend and I kept smiling at each other. We were so happy that the evening was going so well. I gave Noah permission to drive me home. We did not kiss after that date, but I felt great and thanked God in my prayers for that evening.

Whenever Noah wasn't working, we talked on the phone for as long as we could use the two-party phone line. This was because other people had the same phone line that we had, but they had a different phone number. We had to listen for a certain ring before we could pick up the phone. Our ring was two short and one long ring. The two party line sometimes allowed us to hear other people's conversations on our phone.

One day after work Noah asked to meet my sister Sally and my brother-in-law with whom I stayed. My sister told me that Noah could come over after supper on Saturday. She then said, "It's about time I meet this young man that you talk so much about." She also said, "If this is what you want, it would be okay." I was so excited!

That evening Noah sat in our front room. Sally served punch and cookies. I had cleaned the house and put out fresh flowers picked from our neighbor's yard.

This new man in my life told us he was the youngest of four brothers and five sisters. His mother had died in Harriston, Mississippi when he was an infant. He was raised by his papa and siblings. They were a close family that stuck together. He was currently living with his father in a rented room and was also in the process of purchasing a duplex with his sister and brother-in-law. Their plan as co-owners was for Noah to live on one side and his sister and brother-in-law to live on the other side. The money that he earned mostly went towards the down payment on that house and room and board until the duplex was renovated. Noah's father was a laborer on construction sites around the city, and Noah worked at Falstaff Beer Brewery and did odd jobs on the side.

I told him more about myself and that I had a daughter, Nell, whom I had left back in Mississippi with my family. I also told him how much I wanted to prepare a place for the both of us to live in New Orleans. My brother-in-law and Noah talked about jobs and news in the city and other stuff. Sally was impressed with the way he shared information so we could get to know him better. She and I shared smiles. The evening went well.

After he left, Sally and I had a mother-daughter like talk. She told me that she thought Mama and Papa would approve of this gentleman. We went to bed. On my knees I prayed and thanked God.

I felt secure with my new love. It was easy to talk with him and share our dreams and plans together. I met his father and some of his siblings who all had jobs and goals. Some were still in Mississippi. Three months had gone by and our love had grown stronger each day. I felt safe and comfortable with this young man. I knew that I wanted to spend the rest of my life with him.

Several months after I started dating Noah, Sally sat me down after I got home from work one evening. She was holding a letter in her hand from my mother and my father. I asked her if my baby was all right. She told me that she and my brother in law were going to move to his hometown, far from our county in Mississippi. I got scared and starting crying. She had written to our mama and papa about why she had to leave New Orleans, and also that I had met a good young man. The letter my parents sent back said she had to send me back home. She showed me the letter from home that one of my sisters had written for Mama and Papa.

I told Noah about what was happening on the phone that night. The next day he came over with a look on his face that showed his fear and concern for what was about to happen. He then said, "I can't lose you! We are going to work this out, and I'm going to show you. Stay here and marry me. I will adopt your daughter, and she will be my first child." He called for

Sally from the other room, and asked her to help him write a letter to my parents saying that he was buying a home and would always work hard to provide for my daughter and me. He asked my papa for permission to marry me in the letter. He told them that he had deep feelings for me, and he was willing to make Nell and me welcome in his home. He then said, "We can go get your daughter when the house is ready. Please say 'yes?' We can work this out. Let me show you."

Sally mailed the letter the next day and started to pack up. It took about three weeks before her husband and she would be leaving New Orleans. In spite of my pleading, she said Mama and Papa had said that I had to go home and that she could not leave me in New Orleans. I was afraid that when I got home my parents were not going to let me return to the man I loved and the many plans we had made for our future. No letter arrived from Mississippi before I had to leave by train.

With the layovers, the train ride took a long time. I traveled alone since my sister and her husband were going in a different direction. I had a long time to think about what I wanted to do. My parents were going to ask what my plans were. Marriage was really what I wanted, especially after being with the man I had loved for so many months. I imagined him being my daughter's father and us making a complete family. I prayed to God to help Mama and Papa make the best decision.

My papa and brother met me at the train station. I had all of my belongings with me and presents for my baby girl. I was glad to see everyone. After catching up on current news and events, we sat down to a big supper and serious family talk. Mama said, "We didn't write back to that fellow of yours until we could find out if he loves you for real. Your sister spoke well of him. Now, talk to us Tot."

I talked about my relationship with his family and how they all treated me well. I was proud to talk about my dreams of Noah adopting Nell. I told them about the house and my jobs. Everyone was quiet while I talked. Papa and Mama didn't take their eyes off of my face the entire time. When I couldn't think of anything else to talk about, they began to ask many questions. Some of the questions they asked were, "Do you think your fellow can support you and your baby? Does he get up in time for work? Does he make sure you don't need for necessary things? Is he honest? Does he believe in God?" There were so many questions I can't remember them all. Then Mama asked, "Do you want to marry this fellow?" I replied, "Yes!"

Tot and Noah, the Love of her Life

We immediately started making plans for my trip back to New Orleans. I planned to return for my daughter after Noah and I had moved in to our half of the duplex. Papa and Mama had my sister write a letter to Noah that night–telling him we had their blessing for marriage. They let him know they were expecting him to keep his word about taking care of my daughter and me. He was told when to expect me back in New Orleans.

The train ride back was filled with happiness and thankful prayer. Noah waited all evening for that train to bring me back to him. When the train arrived in New Orleans, I walked out of the train door and got to the top step. There he was! He grabbed me in his big arms and lifted me up past the bottom steps. We kissed and he said, "I thought once you returned to Mississippi you wouldn't come back to me. When I hadn't heard from you for a week, I got scared and didn't think you were coming back." It was then that I knew I had made the right decision to return to New Orleans, because he was at the train station when I arrived and was just as happy to see me as I was to see him.

13

Challenges and Successes

After several months of living in rented rooms, our duplex was ready. It was uptown, in the central part of the city on Seventh Street. We had a living room, one bedroom, a kitchen, bathroom, and a small back yard. I loved it! My sister-in-law and her husband moved on the other side of the double house. Noah's father, Richard, moved in with us, which was somewhat of a disappointment at first, because Noah hadn't told me that his father would be living with us. I called Noah's father "Papa" which is what his other children called him. Papa was kind to me, and I got use to having him around. He helped us, and we also helped him. Papa, or Papa Richard, worked at different construction sites in the city. For many years he slept on a fold up bed on one side of the kitchen.

The business arrangement that Noah and his brother-in-law had was well planned. His sister and brother-in-law were not only family but good neighbors and friends as well. It made me so comfortable to know they were close by. I always had family around, even though my own family no longer lived in New Orleans. Noah's family was large and very supportive. Our love grew stronger each day, and we enjoyed being together. We rode the public service bus until we were able to buy a car. Times were hard, but we managed with the income we earned. I knew I would have to hurry to make our home ready for Nell. We bought furniture for our bedroom, and a sofa bed for her to sleep on in the living room.

Noah was working at Falstaff Beer Brewery when I learned that I was pregnant. We were both eighteen years old when he said, "Let's get married." Noah changed the spelling of his last name after we married. He added an extra "L" at the end of his last name. The marriage ceremony took place in our minister's home, and my sister-in-law and her husband, Noah's brother, were witnesses. She and I had married two brothers, and we remain best friends to this day. She was mature, and she knew more about raising children than I did. She also had a son who was older than my daughter Nell.

I often lay awake at night and thought about how God had worked things out for our lives: my meeting Noah, falling in love, Noah wanting to marry me, buying this home, and Noah wanting to adopt my daughter were divine grace.

My second pregnancy was very different than the first. Every month I went to Charity Hospital for prenatal checkups. I took vitamins and learned a lot about what to expect. Even though this was not my first pregnancy, I still had so much to learn. I gained a lot of weight, and my abdomen became extremely large. The doctors said that the baby had a strong heart beat. There were no ultrasound machines for pregnant women in those days.

We planned to put a bassinette in our bedroom for the new baby until the baby could share the sofa-bed with Nell. Papa Richard was still sleeping in the kitchen. I was so happy with the way things were going.

On December 22, 1952 I began having labor pains and was taken to Charity Hospital. My sister-in-law was with me, because Noah was at work. This experience at the hospital was so different than my experience in 1948 with the midwife at home in Mississippi. I was still just as scared and excited to get to see my new baby. Some people said if you carry your baby low in your abdomen it will be a boy, and if you carry it high, it would be a girl. When the doctor said, "Now push hard," I did and delivered a girl with no hair on her head. The doctor began pushing on my abdomen for the afterbirth to come out, and then he said, "Here comes another baby!" The surprise was identical twin girls with all of their fingers and toes and bald heads. They were beautiful red girls who looked just like Noah. My sister-in-law called Noah's job, and he was in the lunchroom waiting for word on the delivery. After he heard about the birth of the twins, he sat down and said, "Lord I have to work two jobs now." The doctors and nurses were cheering and holding the cleaned babies for me to see. I had a natural childbirth, but the doctors had given me medication to ease the pain after the delivery. I prayed and thanked God until I went to sleep.

I let the nurses and doctors name the twins, because I had only planned for one baby and only had one name picked out. The twins were named Joyce and Joy. They came home on Christmas Eve to meet their big sister Nell and their grandfather, Papa Richard. Noah was so proud of his new babies. He also considered Nell to be his own four-year-old daughter. My husband's niece came from Mississippi to help take care of us for a month until my health grew stronger.

14

Building Our Future

Our hope was built on our faith in God. Noah and I had a love that was growing stronger each and every day. Even though we didn't have a lot of material things, we were happy. I served a lot of canned pork 'n beans, and we made ends meet.

Driven by the need to improve our lives, the men in our family all helped to renovate our three-room, shotgun double house. They built two apartments above the double house, one on each side. Noah, his brothers, and brothers-in-law all had so much talent and skills with their hands. Together they built our family homestead.

Our expenses were now mounting with three young children, and Noah's father was still sleeping on a cot in the kitchen. I was not working, but Noah took moonlight jobs whenever he could. We learned to stretch a dollar and save money too. We were proud of our savings account. I looked forward to occasional nights out at Falstaff's Hotel

Entertainment, which was located around the corner from our home. There were family fish fries, barbeques, and fundraising suppers that I also enjoyed. I eventually learned to be a good cook by combining what I learned growing up in the country in Mississippi and from new friends in New Orleans.

We were so happy when Noah came home with news that he had been hired by the Kaiser Aluminum Plant. His new job provided us with family health benefits, a pension, and so much more income. Kaiser Aluminum had also hired several other men in Noah's family. Thank you Jesus!

Noah and I eventually purchased his sister and brother-in-law's half of the double house, and they moved out. We now owned both sides of the duplex and the apartments above each duplex. We began collecting rent from the three apartments connected to our duplex. The extra rent money helped us to buy a new car, and eventually we were able to buy a second car for me.

A Baptist church was built directly across the street from our home. We joined the new church and became friends with the new young minister, Reverend Washington. The Reverend baptized the twins and their cousin on Good Friday. Our twins were later christened by Reverend Washington and his wife. After many years, the congregation of the church eventually divided and moved from the Seventh Street address to its new location on Washington Avenue, several blocks from our home. We later became founding members of the new Guiding Light Baptist Church. Our lives were being built on a solid foundation.

15

My Girls

Education has always been important to my husband and me. Sharecropping did not let my mother and my papa attend school regularly, but they made us promise that we would see to their grandchildren completing their education. I knew that for our girls to be successful in life, they had to have a good family, love, attend church, and finish school.

I did not work outside of the home when my girls were very young. Extra money was earned from the ironing that I took in. By the time Nell and the twins were school age I was able to go back to work.

Nell was four years older than Joyce and Joy. Even at a young age Nell proved to be responsible and helpful. She was wise for her young age, and I knew that I could depend on her. I often left her in charge of the twins when I had errands to run or when they played in the back yard. Papa Richard was still living in the house, so he helped too. Nell seemed as though she were born to be a big sister. The twins, however, were a challenge for everyone. They got into everything. Because they were very active and noisy, it was not easy to keep up with them. Their big sister knew how to keep the twin's behavior in line, and would always "tell Mama." Nell had authority over them when she babysat and often recommended punishment when the twins needed it.

My oldest daughter was quiet and serious about life. Her hobbies were reading all sorts of books and magazines. She went to the library with her friends often. When she was older she loved to shop. She was a dreamer who knew that she wanted to be successful in life. She always had excellent grades in school and never gave us problems. In her young adult life she worked to help pay her way through Xavier University in New Orleans. Her professional academic achievements included earning two master's degrees.

Joyce and Joy were my "butterball" babies. To tell them apart, everyone looked for a black mole on Joy's forehead. Sometimes Noah called both of them "Joyce." They grew up both answering to that name when he called them. I always dressed them alike from their underwear to their dresses; because that's the way I thought it had to be. After bathing them and dressing them in clean clothes to go somewhere, the twins would have Louisiana black dirt on their faces, hands, and clothes soon after.

Everywhere we took the twins people stared or asked questions such as, "How do you tell them apart? Do they cry and need a diaper change at the same time? Do they both feel pain when one is hurt? Is one more active than the other one?"

The twins were in the same classroom until the third grade. Tommy Lafon Elementary, the school they attended, had a policy that twins could not be enrolled in the same classroom. This was a good plan, because they did each other's class work and talked too much in class. Their first grade teacher had permission to spank them when they needed it. She also helped me for many years with the twins' education. Most of the teachers were involved with my twins and with Nell throughout their school years.

Joyce and Joy were both very talented. They were involved in school: cheerleading, dance, majorettes, gymnastics and drill teams. They attended a local music school for singing and dancing lessons. The girls were very popular because of this. Joy loved to sing and Joyce loved to draw and paint. In junior high school they had an identity problem, so I stopped making them dress alike. They also had some of the same friends but began having a few different friends. All of my girls' friends visited our home regularly. The twins made good grades that probably would have been better if they weren't involved in so many activities.

After high school, Joyce received a college scholarship where she earned a bachelor's degree from Mississippi Valley State University, while Joy worked her way through college to earn her bachelor's degree from Southern University. Joyce is a retired teacher from the New Orleans Public School system, and Joy is currently a paralegal specialist.

Noah's father moved out when I learned I was expecting my fourth baby. Maria, the shy one, was born around the corner from our home at Flint Goodridge Hospital on July 3, 1959, a day before her father's birthday. She had a full head of hair, and was beautiful all over. During that time Noah was working the graveyard shift, and he received a raise in salary at the aluminum plant. He got to spend more time with Maria while she was an infant through toddler age than he had with the other girls. The family always teased that Maria was a spoiled daddy's girl. Noah gave her most things she wanted, not just what she needed. Maria was always a good baby and easy to care for. Her three older sisters enjoyed playing with her and combing her beautiful long hair. In her adult life, she too, received a college scholarship and earned both a bachelor's and a master's degree.

Just as Maria was starting kindergarten I learned that we would be having our fifth baby. Noah and I were surprised but happy. That year was filled with both excitement and grief. We were expecting our new baby, but I also had the sadness of my mother's death. After Mama died, Papa moved to Reno, Nevada to live with my sister Bill and her husband. We also had several other family members living there, and Papa was getting too old to try to work a farm. Bill, who had a good paying job at Harold's casino, was better able to care for Papa. She and her husband Jim took care of Papa as well as some of our other family members.

We tried to keep in touch with Papa after he moved to Reno. Because it was expensive to make long distance calls, we didn't talk by phone much. We mostly wrote letters and sent packages through the mail. My sister wrote many letters telling us how Papa was doing. Papa even got to visit New Orleans a few times.

As my husband and I prepared for a new addition to our family, we also made plans to move into a newly purchased, five room double home with a porch and large back yard located in the New Orleans Seventh ward. A family continued to rent the other side of the newly purchased home even after we bought it. We moved into the larger home when my newest baby, Mary, was one month old.

Mary was born on September 6, 1963 at Flint Goodridge Hospital. She was a beautiful baby with a peaceful spirit. Her big sister Nell asked to name her, and we all agreed that she could. My four older girls played with Mary every chance they got, when they weren't in school. They dressed her up, sometimes twice a day, just like she was their baby doll. She loved me to push her on the swing in our new back yard. After living in our new home for two years, we had to move from the Seventh ward because of the new bridge that was going to be constructed right where our house was located. When we moved, Mary made many friends, but she seemed to always have time to spend with the elderly people in our new neighborhood. She brought school friends home all the time. In her spare time, she often visited the older people and shopped for them at the store around the corner. As her sisters got older and left for college or moved away, she became well known for assisting the elderly on our block. To this day, Mary still visits and prays with the elderly as a part of her ministry. She would attend church alone, if I could not go with her. My baby girl never caused problems at home or at school. She always made good grades, and she earned a degree in early childhood development. She married her childhood boyfriend, and they both live with their family in New Orleans.

My girls were raised to fear God and not judge people by the color of their skin. When we visited Lincoln Beach, which was the only amusement park for colored people, they asked about the big roller coaster that could be seen off in the distance. This roller coaster was at the Ponchatrain Beach Amusement Park, and colored people were not allowed to enter or use this park. We simply told them that people were getting the Ponchatrain Park ready for us. The girls questioned why they could not drink from certain water fountains when we went to get groceries. They all spent summers in rural Mississippi with relatives and were sheltered from many racial problems. I am proud of how all my girls turned out and love them very much.

16

Making It

One of the signs that we were "making it" was the opportunity I had to travel. I loved traveling out west, where I experienced driving on roads before there were expressways. We visited the Hoover Dam, which appeared to drop straight down as though it were going on forever. I saw beautiful mountains, Lake Tahoe, Carson City, and Virginia City. It was amazing to see where John Wayne and other cowboys made their movies, and to see horseshoes, saddles, and all the equipment they worked with. I saw the silver dollar lady, and I still have the belt made of silver dollars. The mountains were so high. It seemed like there was no ground on the bottom when we stood at the top of the mountain. I still have family who live in the mountain areas and in Denver, where some of my beautiful grandchildren and great-grandchildren live. I try to visit them often, but over time my allergies and the high altitude begin to create problems for me. Because of my allergies, I don't get to visit them as often as I would like to.

During one of my visits to Reno, I had a chance to visit San Francisco. My sister paid a driver to drive us from Reno to San Francisco. She wanted me to see the crookedest street in America. We ate lunch outside looking over the water with Alcatraz in the background. It was a sunny day, and riding the beautiful, red San Francisco trolley was quite a wonderful experience. The red trolley made me think of the streetcars and our home in New Orleans.

Noah and I got to enjoy life more than we ever had before. He joined a social club and enjoyed the many new friends we made. Noah loved to entertain in our home. I enjoyed cooking many special dishes to please our guests.

Tot and Noah at a Social Event

We were collecting rent from the double or four-plex uptown on Seventh Street and from the apartment next door to us in our Seventh ward house. We never had a problem keeping the apartments rented. We purchased another luxury car and knew where our blessings came from. We continued to attend and enjoy the many social parties that we were invited to. And, it was now time to plan our next goal.

Tot and Noah at a Black-Tie Party

Our lives were really going well, when we got notice that many people in our block had to move to make way for a new interstate highway that was going to be built. A large concrete pillar now stands in the spot where our home was. The government gave us one year to find somewhere else to live, and bought us out. We had to do some quick decision making, because we had only been in our new home for two years.

After searching for a new place to live, we found a two-story home uptown in the lower garden district of New Orleans, now called central city. The neighborhood was racially mixed and quiet. The house had an above ground open basement, living room, dining room, three bedrooms, two bathrooms, and a kitchen. It also had a garage and driveway. During this phase of my life, I was now happily married, the mother of five beautiful girls, and both my husband and I were venturing off into becoming entrepreneurs. This third house offered the potential for both of our dreams to come true. Noah's dream was to have a taxicab business, and my dream was to open a nursery school.

One day my sister called to say that Papa was very sick, and had to be hospitalized. He was suffering with a bladder problem and high blood pressure. She said that Papa was always asking for me and wanted to see me. Bill called me to say that I needed to start getting up there to Reno as soon as I could because Papa was extremely sick, and he was still asking to see his Tot.

My husband and I discussed it and arranged for my sister-in-law to keep the children so that I could leave to go to see Papa. A couple that had always been our friends helped us drive the trip from New Orleans to Reno in our Cadillac. Throughout the trip I called Bill from every gas station we stopped at to find out how Papa was doing. On each phone call Bill said, "Please hurry. He is asking, 'Is my baby here yet?'" When we finally got to the hospital, Papa had passed on. I was so sorry and kissed him on his face. He had tried to wait for my arrival but went home to glory a few hours before we arrived.

We stayed in Reno for the funeral which was nicely done. I met many nieces, cousins, and some in-laws for the first time. Papa was buried in Reno, but I believe his soul rests in Heaven. I loved Papa so much and miss him dearly.

A few years after Papa's death, I began to actively pursue my dream of owning my own daycare business. At that time, my oldest daughter Nell was in high school; the twins were in junior high, and the two younger girls were in elementary school. All of the girls were inviting their friends to our home. There were many times their friends' parents would ask if their own daughters could sleep over because they felt comfortable that boys were not allowed around or in our home. I guess you could say I was like the "Kool-Aid Mom" in our neighborhood, where the parents knew that their children were going to be safe.

My family and friends encouraged me to finally open the nursery school I was always talking about. Noah was very supportive of my dream. He oversaw the renovations of the open basement that later became the location for my nursery school. My girls did the research, and I made many phone calls and trips to City Hall to get information on opening a daycare school. I also visited numerous nurseries and daycare centers and interviewed the owners. At that time there was a great need for licensed day care centers.

After our home and basement renovations passed the health, safety, and fire inspections, I received my occupational license and approval to open my own nursery school. The state approved me for twenty-eight to thirty children. Joyce and I went to the community college to get certified in early childhood education. I named the nursery school using my given middle name, "Lee's Day Care Center." The school had a center wall that divided two classrooms and another wall that separated the kitchen. I hired qualified teachers, ordered the best workbooks and had a very active parent and teacher organization.

The teachers at the elementary school near our home recommended my nursery school to their students' parents, and several of the teachers even had their own children enrolled. Business was good, and I had a waiting list most of the time. I was the director, cook, play pal, and transportation provider. Monday through Friday, I picked children up from all over uptown and brought them to school for educational activities, two hot meals, and a snack. The children were provided a good education. My teachers had the toddlers and pre-school children reading and able to recognize words before they went to first grade. The curriculum included taking the children on various fieldtrips and producing plays on the nursery room stage that Noah built. Our nursery school parents loved the children's presentations.

While operating Lee's Day Care Center, I was cast for a small part in a movie. I auditioned and was selected to work with actors, Kathleen Turner and Dennis Quaid in a movie filmed in New Orleans that was titled *Cloak and Diaper*. Sometime later, we were notified that the title of the movie had been changed to *Undercover Blues*, and the part I had filmed was cut from the final release. The next role I auditioned and was chosen for was to be a look-a-like for Esther Rolle, an actress who played the character "Florida" in the television shows *Maude* and *Good Times*. The auditions took place at the Roosevelt Hotel in downtown New Orleans. There were numerous photographers taking pictures of me in various profiles on the stage. Because the Day Care Center was still open, I decided that the role was not for me, so I declined it. As the owner and director of Lee's Day Care Center, I had to always be available to the children and their parents, so I knew that the role wasn't for me. Sometime later, I received a call from the site asking me why I had not sent the pictures they had requested.

Lee's Day Care Center closed after sixteen successful years. None of my daughters wanted to take it over, because they had their own careers. I was getting tired, and three government nurseries opened in my area. My grandchildren, who also participated in the nursery school activities, began calling me "Mrs. Cruell, just like the other nursery school children. I had to remind them that I was their "grandmother" and not just "Mrs. Cruell."

After closing the childcare center, I began going back to school and work. I went to school four days a week, while I worked five days a week. I was later hired by my lawyer's mother to be on her staff as a caretaker. She had four employees working for her, in addition to a cook who had worked with her for over twelve years. I worked with her for only eight months because of my school schedule. My shift was from three to midnight, but I was allowed to quit my shift at eleven rather than midnight. One afternoon when I arrived at work, she sat me down and told me there was nothing for me to do. I wasn't sure what she meant, I thought that I was being replaced. After we finished talking and because of her caring nature, she said that I should do my homework. Rather than lay me off because there was nothing that needed to be done, she said that she wanted me to be her designated driver. She also wanted me to take her to her doctor's appointments and to be the only one to bank her money. She had a dress shop, and her daughter brought clothes for her to try on. She never tried on anything before I saw it. Her other employees always asked if they could help her with the clothes. They often said, "Bertha, see what she likes first. You are the only one that she wants to help her." She was a special employer who looked after and took care of me.

While I was a student and also worked as a caretaker, Noah was able to secure a Certificate of Public Necessity and Convenience to operate a taxicab business. He eventually owned seven taxicabs. Noah did most of his own auto mechanic work and even drove one of the cabs to earn extra money when he wasn't working on his job at Kaiser Aluminum. We were *making it*.

17

The Lord Is My Shepherd

At an early age I learned so much, and I never thought I was being used by my husband, because I was so much in love. I thought I was a good little wife. My family was my life, and Sunday was our favorite day. On Sundays I looked forward to being together with my family, and the girls looked forward to being with their father. Sunday was our family day. Then, there was a change; Noah started to ask me to pack a bag for him on Fridays, because he wanted to go to visit his brother. It was okay the first time I packed a bag. It was neat for that weekend, and he came home that Sunday. The second time I packed a bag for him, I got a funny feeling, something just didn't feel right. Something happened that made me cry. I said, "You ran all my girlfriends away, and you've got it all. Oh no, it doesn't go like that, I don't want you to go. Your bag is packed, walk out the door." I then said to myself, "What am I doing? Am I crazy?" He knew I was angry. "No," I said to myself, "I'm not crazy." I then said, "I hope you go off in the river." This conversation took place on a Friday. On the following Sunday before he returned, I was notified that he was in the hospital. He had driven into a river. I notified his family of what happened, and they went to get him. He returned Sunday night with a bandaged head. The next time he left, I packed his bags again. This was the third and last time. I cried and told him, "Please don't leave me." I then told him, "I hope you wreck that Cadillac car." On Sunday night of that weekend he wrecked the car, two blocks from the house. The car was demolished. That Sunday night, he couldn't even walk the two blocks to our house. From then on, he always told me, "Please don't tell me what you hope happens to me again."

Our extended family had always been close. All of the children and cousins were close in age and usually played together. We gathered together regularly for family fish fries, suppers, and just to have fun at each others' homes. My girls loved their father's sisters and brothers like extended parents. They visited some of the aunts and uncles in Mississippi every summer.

It was a few years before I closed the nursery that I noticed a change in my husband. The love of my life no longer lay in bed with me talking. He stayed out until late at night and would not be at work. If I asked him where he had been, he cursed me. It seemed that every month when I received a government check for state assigned nursery students, he asked me for money to buy taxicab parts and pay bills. I learned that he was not paying the bills. Instead, he said he needed it all to keep his cabs running because a driver had not paid the cab rental fees. He always had an excuse to demand my money. On many occasions, when we argued over money, he would hit me. The girls heard us arguing, and he didn't care. In the middle of the night Noah often left our bed and our home with no reason given to me. I was now afraid of him. I was informed that my husband had become a regular dice player.

My husband had a hot temper, and sometimes it got completely out of control, which led him to fight me. I could have left him, but decided not to because he had done so much to help me, including hiring a cleaning person who came into our home once a week to help keep our home clean. He also provided me with the best of everything, and he made me feel like no request was too large.

I could not talk to my girls about how I was feeling, nor could I talk to Noah's sisters because my relationship with them had changed. My sister-in-law, his oldest brother's wife was always close to me, and she was the only adult I could talk to. We often prayed together, and she also offered support. My own sisters were scattered around the country, and I did not want to burden them with my problems.

All five of my daughters were still living at home and enrolled in school, when one night the phone rang. One of them answered the phone and said, "Mama, it's for you." A woman was on the other end, and she called me a "fool." She said that I was working to make the home ready for her to move into, because she said Noah was "her man." When Noah came home I asked him who she was, and he lied that night. This was the beginning of a lot of verbal and physical abuse. He told the few friends that I still had to not ask me to go out with them. I was afraid of my husband. He controlled my every move. There were many times he came home drunk, and one time he stayed away for a week.

I want my grandchildren and great-grandchildren to know the truth about the struggles I went through. My daughters were already aware of the truth about the abuse and violence in our home. On many Sundays there were huge fights between Noah and me. Sometimes I wondered what we were fighting about. He often commented to me, "Why do you always leave for church when I come home?" And, when I returned home from church, he would then say, "Why are you so late?" My answer was usually, "I spoke to the pastor at the end of the church service." Noah became so angry, he went berserk. He asked me

"Why does the pastor want to talk to you?" I answered, "He stands outside after the service to talk to all of his members." On one particular Sunday, after I changed from my church clothes to my regular house clothes, Noah went to the closet and removed my beautiful church dress and proceeded to cut it up. I screamed at him, "You are a walking devil." That Sunday our fight was bigger than ever.

At this time, Noah was rarely attending church services with me. I always asked him to join me, and he usually declined. He came from a church-going family, and all of the men in his family were deacons. On one of my Communion Sundays he came home with alcohol on his breath. In preparing for church, I went into my room where I had laid my white usher's uniform on the bed, and the dress was not there. I asked Noah, if he knew where my dress was. He replied, "Look for it!" He had put it away where I wouldn't find it. I was very upset, and this led to another huge fight.

Of all the members of Noah's family including his father, sisters, and brothers, he was the only one with a hot temper. His behavior was also disturbing to my girls. Sometimes they came home and told me how their father had taken them to a lady's house, when they thought they were going to be spending a fun day out with their dad. They did not like that. And, at ten-years-old and younger, the girls did not understand.

There were times they asked me, "Who is that woman?" I did not know how to answer that question. I started to question him about it, because our girls needed to know the truth. They loved their father so much. They thought he could do no wrong. He was their joy.

As time went on, Noah accused me of turning the girls against him, which I never would have done. I had never in my life personally experienced violence until Noah became an abusive husband. My parents never touched each other in a non-loving or violent manner. I had grown up in a warm and loving home environment. I thought that I had to stay in this marriage and this household, because I did not know any better at the time. My mother had never left Papa or her family.

Because I stayed in this situation far too long, it affected our daughters in many ways. Two of my daughters divorced twice, and three are still married with great husbands. After living in our home and watching how I was lied to, abused, and disrespected, the girls learned what does and does not make a happy home. Because of the abuse and violence, I will never have a man put his hand on me like that again. I stayed in this situation longer than I should have because I was thinking more about the girls, and not enough about me. One thing our daughters have said is that they will never stay in a marriage for the sake of the children. My daughters and I have learned that if we do not take care of ourselves, then we cannot take care of our children.

I still have terrible nightmares! Sometimes we forget the power in faith. Whenever I say "Jesus," it brings me to tears. That's what faith does to me. I thought I needed therapy. My faith was the answer. In a dream one night, I saw my mother coming down in white from a cloud. She took her hand, and anointed my forehead. I opened my eyes, and she was gone. Faith brought me through, and I am still standing. The Lord is my Shepherd!

I have to talk about the new faith that God gave me, He never fails. He let me know that He will never leave me. He did not. He was there in spirit the first night I was ever alone. Our uptown house was a large home with tall French shutter doors and windows. I could never get the fear out of my mind as I stood in front of those tall windows as they shook one evening. That night I heard someone shaking and rattling the outside shutter doors, asking for a person who didn't live in the house. Everyone was asleep; my husband answered the door as I stood behind him. The stranger asked if someone lived there by a certain name that we did not know. I could see through the window that there was one man on the porch, and two other men were standing in the street underneath a tree. I was afraid they would come back when I was alone.

A few nights later, while my husband was at work, and my daughters were at a sleepover, I was left at home all alone. I walked from door to door; I had never been so afraid. Not thinking of what God had said, "Wherever you are, I am also," I was very tired. I went in the bedroom, locked the door, and prayed. I was so afraid. I told God, "I am a woman, please take this fear away." I was still awake around one o'clock in the morning. The last time I remember being awake was at two o'clock. This is the way I slept in spirit. I lay on my back, and God was on the right of me sitting in a chair holding my wrist. He took his right hand and laid it on my right wrist. That is all I remember. At six o'clock the next morning I woke, opened the door and walked out. I was never afraid after that. I used to only be afraid of the sick and darkness, but God healed me of all of those fears. I am no longer afraid.

After making it through my night of fear, with God's help, I became a real businesswoman. I kept records of all of the nursery school bills, teachers' salaries and expenses. I paid the house bills on time, paid my church tithes, and collected rent from the apartments. Noah took care of the taxi business and otherwise continued to provide what we needed. He did not have access to my new bank account, and he also knew not to ask me for money for his taxi business. Our lives had changed. The girls asked me to leave Noah. I chose not to leave him, because I didn't want my girls to have to change their home and schools and possibly not have a chance to finish their goals to be successful in the future.

Time passed, and I began to feel that things were no longer violent, but my marriage had changed. Once, after the older girls had married or moved away for college, the telephone rang, and I answered it. There was a woman on the phone who asked to speak to my husband, and I gave him the phone. After he got off the telephone I questioned the conversation, and he became violent again.

After so much disrespect and violence, I decided it was time to leave. I had no family in town for me to go to. Noah's family was the only family I knew. There was no place for me to stay because he could walk in at any time he decided. I went to stay at his cousin's house (a cousin he didn't see often). I stayed with her for four days. Then, on Friday night when I was in the living room with the lights off looking at television, the doorbell rang. I could not see who was at the door. When I opened it, all hell broke out! Noah grabbed my arm and pulled me out of the house and onto the porch. He kept saying, "You don't have to stay here. You have a home." There was so much going on that his cousin and the next-door neighbor, along with the neighbor's family, came out. To protect himself, his family, and me, the next-door neighbor armed himself. Noah grabbed me and said, "Come here now." In the meantime, Noah's cousin was trying to protect me. When Noah pulled out a knife, his cousin took a garbage can top to fight him off, but he wounded her with the knife. By the time the police arrived, Noah had gone. I stayed all night with his cousin in the hospital. I had never before felt so guilty, because I felt that her injuries were my fault. I told her, "It should have been me in the hospital. You tried to help me," and it was not a good feeling. She never let me take the blame, but I knew better. I stayed with her and took care of her until she got better. I found out later that a friend of Noah's had hidden him, and the police were never able to find him. That's when I knew I had to do something. Noah left our home and said that he was never coming back.

My daughter Joyce made an appointment for me to see a lawyer. After visiting with the lawyer, we learned that I could get a peace bond and that I could also press criminal charges against my husband. I felt that Noah would kill me if I sent him to jail. I decided to file for divorce. During that time I learned that the woman who had caused so much hurt to my family and me was introduced to my husband by one of his own family members, and that they had entertained both of them in their homes. I no longer trusted some of his family, who I had always thought cared for me like their own family. His brother's wife and two of his sisters were the only ones I trusted.

After a few weeks Noah showed up at our home crying and begging for forgiveness. He asked me to stop the divorce proceedings. The next day, I called my lawyer, who was the son of a family that I had taken care of shortly after I arrived in New Orleans. The lawyer wanted to see my daughter and me in his office. We stayed in consultation with the lawyer for a long time. He told me that if things did not change for the better that we only needed to make one call to him, and he would start the divorce proceedings immediately. He did not charge me for any services.

Today, I understand the power of forgiveness. I could have let hatred for Noah and everyone involved eat me up, but Jesus hates the sin and not the sinner. I loved my husband and always kept my vows. I could not give up on him, and I felt obligated to raise my daughters in a family where both parents were present. As a result of this, all of my girls became successful, educated women. The Lord is my Shepherd!

18

The Front Porch Swing

We hired my brother-in-law to build this huge porch swing that had a wide seat and a high leaning back. It was so wide that you could sleep on it. The swing was made with thick birch wood. It was bolted to the stud beams of the fourteen-foot high porch ceiling. The ceiling also had an outdoor fan to keep us cool while swinging.

Our porch swing was special to my family and many others. It hung on our large concrete front porch, high off the sidewalk, about thirteen steps above the ground level. While sitting in the big swing, you could see straight down the block on both sides of our street. If you stood on the top step of the stairs leading up to the front door, you could see into the next block. I planted a large Japanese Magnolia tree in the center of my beautiful flower garden, just below the porch. The tree gave shade and housed many birds which made for a relaxing and peaceful summer sitting on the swing.

My fondest memories of the porch swing are of the weekends, when I worked in my flower garden. I, like my mother, had a "green thumb." When I sat on the porch swing watching the huge magnolia tree in my front yard, I was able to see the seasons change, watch the butterflies flutter, and smell the aroma of all of the fresh flowers, including the blossoming azaleas and the jasmine around the tree. The fragrance of the flowers was sweet like perfume. I was always able to enjoy the swing while working in the garden or while peacefully swinging in the cool of the evening.

Just like chicken soup is good for colds and what ails you, my porch swing was like medicine to many who had the pleasure of sitting on it. It was great for a relaxing, quiet time for praying, thinking, conversing, and talks with the children. A lot of gossip, ice cream and icebergs were shared there. Even romantic kisses took place there; just ask my girls and grandchildren. Noah used to take a pad and pillow out there for long naps in the summer and fall seasons.

One of our neighbors once told us someone was sleeping on the porch at night. My husband went out the next night and found a man sitting in the swing. Noah gave the man food, clothes, and a little money. To our knowledge, the man never returned after that. Our neighbors, however, told us that they had seen other strangers on our porch swing when we were not home. Once a lady was walking by and looked up to speak to me as I sat on the swing. She asked if she could join me. We had a nice conversation and became friends. She did not live in the neighborhood, but she had seen the porch swing and said it reminded her of her swing in the country. Many friends were made on that swing. The mailman, who walked from house to house and other delivery people even used the popular swing for a quick rest.

There were a couple of times the swing created real drama. On one occasion the chain on one side of the swing broke under the weight of three very large adults, and I was one of them. Thank God no one was injured, we were only embarrassed. One side of the swing had fallen onto the concrete porch with the swingers all on top of each other. Later we laughed about it. For days the children asked, "When are we going to get the swing fixed?" Noah and his brother-in-law bought heavier chains and put the swing back up.

The second dramatic situation took place when four of the grandchildren were having a good time as all four of them were playing and swinging really high. While inside of the house near the front entrance, I, along with the kids' parents, heard a loud crash and screams. According to one of my older granddaughters, the swing broke and crashed against the porch railing directly behind it just as the fifth child had jumped on the swing, mid-swing. After that incident, the swing was demolished and not repairable. That was the end of our porch swing. The children's parents offered to buy me another one, but I would not allow them to. That particular swing was special and was irreplaceable. We didn't want a store bought swing.

Word spread that the swing was gone, and many friends and families tried to get me to change my mind to not replace it. I didn't realize how important that swing was to so many people. The first Mardi Gras after the swing was gone, many visitors shared their stories about the swing. I decided that the swing dramas were a warning and a blessing.

19

Sons After All

My sons-in-law were the sons Noah and I did not have naturally. All of them entered the family knowing how close we were. I love them all, and they have always returned the love. Rules were very strict with the first three girls courting, but we loosened up with the last two girls.

Several of the courting rules in our home:

- No phone calls from boys were permitted until the girls were fourteen years old.

- Boys had to ask my husband or me to visit the house.

- No dating was allowed until age fifteen (school functions were acceptable).

- A little sister or another family member had to be in the room or adjourning room when one of the girls had a boy guest.

- I usually spoke to the girls' teachers and the boys' family member.

- A two-hour date was long enough.

- The girls were never allowed to visit a boy's house.

- After age fifteen, dating was permissible in a group or at school functions until the girls turned sixteen, at which time they were allowed to date without chaperones or being in a group.

At one time Noah was a very large man, and was known to be over-protective of his five daughters. People often said, "If a boy got to visit more than two or three times and was still not afraid of my Mr. Cruell, then they had a chance to court one of his daughters."

The younger girls were allowed to have their boyfriends visit the family on weekends. For the three older girls, the boys really spent time with us as a family rather than sitting on the sofa with little sisters present. This way the younger boys started off learning to enjoy being part of our gatherings.

After his daughters' weddings, Noah helped all of his sons-in-law by giving of himself in so many ways. He always made sure to help if they needed a car or a job. He taught several of them about carpentry, handyman work, auto mechanics, construction, minor electrical and plumbing, major appliances and small appliances repair as well as managing money. They also learned about our taxicab business and our nursery school business. They always knew they would have our unconditional love, respect, and financial support if needed. We never interfered in their marital matters and didn't take sides.

20

Christmas in New Orleans

Every year our family had an annual Christmas gathering, gift exchange, and family dinner tradition, which started after my daughters became adults and had their own families. Each year we pulled names from a box and exchanged gifts at a large family brunch held at one of our homes. On Christmas Eve, the girls came over to wrap last minute gifts. Joy always took the grandchildren out caroling at our neighbors' homes in the block. While they were out, I prepared eggnog and cookies that were served after they returned.

Our Christmas tree was always tall and full of beautiful lights, garland, and traditional ornaments. The mantelpiece was decorated with stockings, candles, and Christmas ornaments. During this time of year the house was filled with laughter, joy, and Christmas music on the radio or television. The children loved to share their wish list for Santa.

On Christmas morning around ten o'clock, the family gathered together for the opening of gifts. We had a continental breakfast together around the tree. Breakfast consisted of doughnuts, juice, and coffee. Each grandchild had a turn to call out the name for each gift. Normally the gift opening and breakfast lasted about two hours, and then each of my girls went home with their families until Christmas dinner later that day.

Christmas dinner was always carefully and beautifully planned. We set the tables with white tablecloths, flowers, china, stemmed glasses, and silver flatware. There was always more than enough food if unexpected guests stopped by. My grandchildren ate at a separate table in the breakfast room, where they watched Christmas shows on television while they ate. As the years went by they often asked, "When will we be old enough to sit at the adult table?" I never cheated them out of a having a beautiful table arrangement. I always decorated their table just as nicely as ours. After dinner, the men helped clean the dishes, and then the games began. We played cards, dominoes, and several board games. Our beautiful Christmas day ended with games that were filled with a lot of laughter, fun, and excitement.

21

Fat Tuesday

Fat Tuesday or Mardi Gras is the annual carnival event for our city. It is one of the largest and most famous celebrations in New Orleans. We lived on a city block where the Mardi Gras Black Indians gathered, and the Zulu Club, which is an African American Social Aid and Pleasure Club, paraded their carnival floats. Their floats and paraders danced and marched right in front of our home which was located only two blocks from St. Charles Avenue. St. Charles Avenue is one of the main street routes for all of the major parades. The Mardi Gras activities and festivities begin a week before Fat Tuesday, and the partying goes on all week.

Each year, during this celebration, we saw some of the same people attending the parades, and our house was always open to them. At six o'clock in the morning, before we even got out of bed, the doorbell rang. People were already outside on our porch swing holding their coolers full of food, water, and liquor. I always prepared a lot of food for our drop-in parade friends, family, and guests. Our guests and we celebrated at the full bar in the basement family room prior to the establishment of the nursery school. After the nursery school began operating in the basement, Noah had built a full bar in the upstairs den of our home where most of the celebrations were held. The den was added after some major renovations had been done on our uptown home. He kept the bar full, stocked with all kinds of drinks and alcohol that any visitor could want. We never ran out of beverages for our guests. If it appeared that we were close to running out of alcohol, Noah quickly ran out to the liquor store to restock the bar.

After the parades were over, our friends and family continued to party and eat. People called our home the "party house," because we entertained a lot. With Noah and I both having our own businesses, we knew many people who would visit us on the weekends, holidays, and during special celebrations. Our family name was known throughout the town. Often, when I was out and about in the city at various locations, someone would approach me and say, "Oh, I was at your home with my friend the other day." I would respond, "Oh really?" This situation had gotten too big, especially if I couldn't recognize someone who had been at my house; so, it had to stop. I talked it over with my husband, and after many beautiful years we stopped the open house during Mardi Gras.

We began to remodel our home again. Noah was good with his hands. He did carpentry work on our home, worked on his own cabs, and also helped all the women, families, and homeowners on our block who needed handyman work done. Noah never failed to help when they needed him, and I never had to call a handyman. The neighbors called him a "jack of all trades." Noah was doing some plumbing on our home when he first started to get sick. One day he said, "Baby, I'm not going to be around here much longer." Gradually his illness became worse, and he was not able to work anymore. He said, "Baby, I have to teach you about the cab business before I go." He then said, "I will work with you. I have got to know if you can operate the business before I leave here." The cabs were always his business, and I was not involved. However, he worked with me daily, and six months later he said, "You are ready!" It was like he knew when he would be crossing over to the other side.

22

Losing Noah

As of the date of these stories, I have been blessed to not have had any serious illnesses, major injuries, or surgeries except for a hip replacement which I have recovered from fully. I did once have an incident with those popular Dutch clog shoes. They caused me to break one of my toes when I fell to the ground a long time ago. Another time, I was jumping up to catch a cabbage from a float at a St. Patrick Day parade, and the big cabbage broke my finger. That finger is still a little crooked today. I didn't go to the doctor early enough because I didn't know it was broken. Except for a few simple cooking burn scars on my forearms and hands, I'm just fine. All good cooks have some burn scars.

After becoming ill, Noah lived with his sickness for quite some time without knowing what it was. Even though he took an annual physical for his job at the aluminum plant, the illness went unnoticed until his elbow was mysteriously inflamed for a week. He tried every home remedy that he knew of or heard of, even vinegar with needles in it and W-D 40 rubs. I finally convinced him to see a doctor. He learned that his blood pressure and sugar level were out of control. He had now been diagnosed with diabetes. This diagnosis changed his life when he was only fifty years old. He had worked every day of his life, and prior to that time had never been admitted to the hospital for a serious illness.

It was difficult for Noah to accept that his lifestyle had to change, and it made him angry. Sometimes he hollered at me for no reason. I prepared his diet food just as his nurse had instructed me to, and he enjoyed it and usually had enough to eat after he got used to the small portions.

Even though he was getting used to the new diet and the small portions, there were so many times where he came home, checked my stove pots, and then called around to our girls to see what they had cooked. He was missing some of the foods that he so much enjoyed. He would then decide to go over to their homes and raid their pots. I began to call and warn them of his coming and tell them to put their food in the freezer. That didn't stop him until he had to go back in to the hospital with high blood pressure. Again, he said he would change his eating habits. Even though he loved good home cooked food, he really did try to change his eating habits after the second hospital visit.

Eventually, we learned that his kidneys had begun to fail. Based on this diagnosis, he had to start dialysis treatments three times a week. In spite of the dialysis treatments making him very weak, he continued to drive one of his cabs and do most of the mechanical work on the cabs. I loved my husband and hated to see him suffer.

The weaker he got, the angrier he became. He refused to stay at the hospital, if I didn't stay with him. Many times I attempted to leave the relationship, but my heart said, "No." On the nights that he stayed in the hospital, I remained by his side. I kept my vows to my husband, and I'm glad I did.

Noah had his first heart attack and spent a week in the hospital for valve work. He was thankful that they did not have to cut his chest open. He recuperated well considering how serious his health was failing. There were times when he couldn't walk through the house without getting short of breath. After each dialysis treatment, he had to stay in bed most of the day because of how weak the treatments made him feel.

As my husband's health began to diminish, so did my sister Bill's leading to a sudden and fatal heart attack. My husband and I, along with our family, flew to Reno to witness the celebration of Bill's life. The funeral was attended by many family and friends who had come from several states.

We lost my loving sister, but we continued to be united as a family. Even though we had a lot of family in the Reno area where Bill had lived, we still had many other extended family members who lived in California, Washington, Michigan, Mississippi, Louisiana, New York and other states. They all had tried to make an honest living far away from the hard life in the cotton fields of the South. We continued to keep in touch through mail, phone calls, and visits.

Shortly after Bill's death, my sister Lula, who had been living in a convalescent home in Reno, became extremely ill and moved in with us in New Orleans, because she did not have children who could care for her. Our relatives who lived in Reno could no longer provide for her. I paid someone to fly with her from Reno to New Orleans so that she could live the rest of her life with Noah and me. Lula told me every day that she knew that the Lord would not leave her to be so lonely in that nursing home. She said that she had been served tasteless and inedible soft food while in the nursing home. Once Lula moved in with us, I was now the main caregiver for two very sick loved ones. Noah, my girls, their husbands, and my grandchildren helped as much as they could with Lula's care. Every week Joyce drove Lula, along with her wheelchair, to some of Lula's favorite places. She enjoyed sitting on the porch swing talking to the many people who passed our home. She thanked me daily for making her happy and caring for her. She was loved by my grandchildren, and she loved them as if they were her own. She was able to use her money to enjoy doing what she never thought she would be able to do again

Lula began losing her memory and could no longer walk using her walker. After living with us for almost two years, she passed away and was buried in the space that had planned for my own body in Mount Olivet Mausoleum. I am grateful that I had a chance to help my sister enjoy the last years of her life, and our family is stronger for the experience.

Not many men have a chance do what my husband did for his family as he was facing a possible early death himself. After his second heart attack, Noah started to settle business matters that would help to make my life less difficult after his death. My eyes swell up with tears when I think of how he tried so hard to make-up for the hard times he had caused our girls and me when he was younger. Noah went to lawyers and notaries to make sure my name was on everything he owned. He explained the workings of the taxi business, showed me how to screen drivers, collect rent, and pay line fees. He painted our home and had a lot of repairs done. He apologized to me many times telling me how sorry he was for putting me through so much pain.

In spite of his past behaviors, Noah was a good man, a good father and a great provider. He insisted that every Sunday his daughters, sons-in-law, and grandchildren come to dinner at our home or that we all go out to dinner at a nice restaurant. He was able to make his last trip to Canton to see my brother, Pete. After many years in New York, Pete had moved back to Mississippi to be with his children and other family. Noah and I were happy to reconnect with my big brother, whom I had not seen in more than thirty years. My daughters, their husbands and children were there for a great family reunion. During the evening of that happy reunion, my husband started to lose his eyesight. When we returned home his doctor said Noah's condition was related to his diabetes, and they adjusted his many medications to try to improve his condition.

On Father's Day, June 2000, Noah said that his gift from his family should be that all of his daughters, their husbands and children should go to Boomtown Casino for a family holiday get together. Noah insisted on picking up the tab for all of the meals, as well as paying for the grandchildren to play in the arcade. The grandchildren loved their grandpa, and he cherished them.

While most of the family was in the serving line waiting to be seated, Joy and I waited in the car with Noah for the food line to get shorter. Even though Noah had his oxygen tank on, he had become extremely weak. My oldest grandson went into the restaurant and alerted everyone that his grandfather had become very ill in the car. Noah insisted that everyone remain at the restaurant, and they were not to worry about him. Joy and I began to return home with Noah in the back seat of the car. I rode in the back seat with him sitting close. He was sweating profusely. On the ride home, Noah told me that he needed to go to the hospital, but he said that he wanted to stop by our house first. When we arrived at our home Noah told me that he, "didn't want to get out of the car," but then said that he, "just wanted to sit and look at our home." He also told me he could not see clearly.

Joy called the hospital and stayed on the cell phone with the emergency room people until we arrived at the hospital. Shortly after Noah was admitted for this, his third heart attack, a "code blue" was called. Noah was leaving us to be with the Lord. He was revived and was able to talk to me. I held his hand and rubbed his face. He was blind but was in his right mind. We talked, and he said he would make it to dialysis the next morning. However, I knew that he probably would not make it to dialysis the next day. Joy called all of our family on their cell phones, and they all arrived at the hospital within a half an hour, at which time the doctors were trying to resuscitate Noah. His death was announced with his daughters and their husbands present. I closed his eyes and kissed him while his body was still warm. We all cried and prayed. Our king and the love of my life had died.

My husband had a beautiful home service preached by his long time friend and Minister of God's word. There was standing room only at the funeral. The repast was held at Joyce's church, where I eventually joined and became a member. Noah is buried next to my sister Lula in Mt. Olivet Mausoleum. I loved my husband, but the Lord loved him best. Family and friends from around the country came to pay their respect and talk about their friendships and good memories. After his death, the neighbors shed many tears as they cried on their porch out front. Noah was a part of their family too. He was a good and well respected man.

23

Betsy, Camille, and Katrina

Hurricane Betsy

Surrounded by water and six feet below sea level, New Orleans has always been fraught with the threat of hurricanes. Hurricane Betsy, which hit the city in September of 1965, was one of the most frightening storms any of us had ever seen. On the day that Betsy was supposed to hit the city, we thought that maybe it had by-passed us, but the next day the warning came too late for us. It had turned around and had come back to devastate New Orleans that night.

It was the longest night I have ever remembered. Many years prior to his death, my husband was working the graveyard shift at Kaiser Aluminum in Chalmette, Louisiana, from 11:00 p.m. to 7:00 a.m. the next morning. My daughters and I were at home in the basement where we sought covered protection in the area underneath the front concrete porch. During those years and at the time of the hurricane, the basement had been rented to a single mother and her daughter. Out of fear, and not knowing what would happen, we all held onto each another. Noah, who was still at work, didn't know if we were dead or alive, and we were thinking the same about him. Through a window in the porch area where we were huddled, we could see light, and people outside with hard hats on their heads. The wind and noise made it seem like the upstairs was coming down upon us. The window glass was popping; crystal chandeliers and ceiling light fixtures were swinging back and forth; and the floodwaters outside looked like a river. Then the lights went out!

The next morning, the wind had stopped, and we were all able to go upstairs. It looked like a tornado had gone through the house. Then, we opened the front door and we saw my husband outside, with both arms straight out wading in water that had risen up to the porch where we had stayed all night. We called out to him, and he yelled back to us that he had "walked all the way." His job was twenty-four miles from home. This brought back memories of having seen a twister when I was about eleven-years-old. I was walking to visit a friend. I was alone and on the dusty road. The ground was very dry, and the sun was big and bright. I experienced something I had seen with my own eyes. There was a wind that came up. I stopped, and looked up. A twister touched down, and round and around, and in minutes it was over. I asked questions about what I saw. It was a whirlwind that no one should ever be in.

When my husband arrived at the door, he had just walked through strong winds, rain, and flood waters. The aftermath of Hurricane Betsy got worse from this point on. We had no lights or electricity, no gas, no food, no ice, no telephone service, and the city was in complete darkness. We sat outside at night trying to keep cool, and we made several trips to the K &B drug store for ice. Noah put my car lights on so that we would have some light for the house. For two weeks the streetlights and the electricity were out. We lost all of our food in the kitchen refrigerator; however, we were blessed to have had a big, long deep freezer filled with food that got us over. My husband and I drove out when we could, and we purchased a generator. There was water, but there was not any gas to use the gas stove. We used the barbeque grill to cook. We shared everything we had with the neighbors and they shared with us. The transistor radio was the only electronics we had to tell us the news. That's when we heard about the many dead bodies that had been found throughout the city. There were a few stores still open, thank God. The Ninth ward of the city was hit the hardest with the floodwaters, broken windows, and blown off rooftops. We lived uptown, but it didn't matter where you lived in the city, everyone was touched by Betsy. I was thankful for having my family safe.

Hurricane Camille

After only a few years recovering from Hurricane Betsy, we got early warning from the news that Hurricane Camille was going to hit the city around midnight on August 17, 1969. With an early warning to the citizens of New Orleans to evacuate the city, my family and I packed our bags and headed for Houston, Texas. We packed three days worth of changing clothes. We booked a hotel in Houston and sat up all night listening to the television to see how the hurricane was going to affect our city. On the third day we returned home. It turned out to be a small vacation for all of us. There had been a change in the path of Hurricane Camille. It made a turn away from the city before it was supposed to hit New Orleans. God blessed us again!

Hurricane Katrina

With early warnings in August 2005, we were fortunate to have left New Orleans two days before Hurricane Katrina hit. My family and I drove in three carloads to the North Dallas, Texas home of my oldest grandson. The drive took us nearly fourteen hours, a trip that normally takes eight hours. Following our stay at my grandson's home, my granddaughter made hotel reservations for all of us at a Dallas hotel, and we checked into the hotel. She had been employed by the same hotel chain in New Orleans while in college. Upon our arrival at the hotel, the managers put my granddaughter immediately to work at the front desk when it was known how much damage Katrina had caused to the city of New Orleans. We paid for three rooms at the hotel. After combining our money to pay for a few more days, FEMA kicked in and covered our remaining hotel stay and food. Everyone was really nice to us.

For hours we all sat together watching TV wondering what was going to happen to us if we didn't have a home to return to. It was a blessing to look around and see my children and grandchildren. We had packed clothes for three days like we always did when we ran from hurricanes. When the television news was finally able to show us the devastation that had happened in New Orleans, we couldn't believe it.

One of my daughter's home had been washed away from its slab and never found. Another daughter had eight feet of water in her home. Two of my other daughters' homes, as well as my own home, had suffered wind damage to the roofs but no flood damage. We were grateful to have left the city when we did.

The churches, along with many Dallas citizens and organizations donated clothes to us during our extended stay there. We were grateful, because we needed extra clothes and had been re-washing the clothes we brought with us. Every day there were tables in the hotel ballroom full of clothes and shoes in all sizes, new personal hygiene articles, snacks, books, and toiletries. Someone was there every Sunday to drive us to church where more supplies were distributed.

When we realized we would be in Texas for an even longer time than we had planned, my daughters all started to look for somewhere else to live besides the hotel. One family rented a townhome, the other two families rented apartments, and one daughter accepted a job transfer to another state, where her company paid for her transportation and room and board. The city of Dallas never stopped giving. We were glad that FEMA helped out, but we knew it would eventually end, so we used our emergency funds wisely and kept receipts. Some of us were getting used to living in Dallas. Several of my family members got jobs to help pay the bills.

Then, the time came for us to return home to New Orleans. I remember the first time we drove into the city. The scenes were like something I didn't think would ever happen in my city. The closer we got to New Orleans it seemed that everything was covered in blue plastic– all over the roofs and buildings. The air had a foul odor, and flies swarmed on us as soon as we got out of the car. I had never seen anything like it. Flies literally landed on your skin, like mosquitoes, and you had to swat them to get them off of you. There were no birds. We saw lots of dead dogs in the streets, and because there was no garbage service, there were lots of green trash bags filled with garbage piled high on the sidewalks and streets. The trees, which were missing their tops, were no longer green or filled with buds or blossoms.

My home had some wind damage, but everything else was the same as I had left it. There were no restaurants opened. We had to drive to Metairie in the suburbs to get food and water. My daughter who had lost her home had lived two blocks from where the levy broke in the lower Ninth ward. She was the one whose job was transferred to another city immediately after Katrina. We tried to cross the bridge to see if we could find her house, but the National Guard would not let us enter the area. Flooded out cars, boats, ambulances, broken furniture, and wood siding were scattered everywhere we drove. Most of the city affected by the floodwaters was surrounded by boarded up houses.

Two of my daughters decided to make their home in the Dallas area. They both bought beautiful homes there and convinced me to sell the family home in New Orleans and move in with them or buy a condo near them. It didn't make sense for me to keep up the large family home, living alone. It had become too much for me to care for which included paying the high property taxes, dealing with the basement apartment renters, hiring and paying repairmen and contractors for the upkeep of the home, and trying to maintain the taxi business in these failing times. A local church bought my family home and most of my furniture after it had been on the market for two years. That was a blessing that I prayed for day and night. After the sale of my home in New Orleans, I moved to Dallas to live with one of my daughters and her family, where I can now live with less stress and worry. Thank God!

24

My New Life

New Orleans was the place where my husband and I raised our children, and I am glad. It's a place where people cared about you and looked out for you if you needed them. Everyone in our neighborhood knew each other and showed their love. I was blessed that my children came up in a neighborhood where everybody looked after the children. I love New Orleans! It's the place where I developed into the woman I am today.

After Hurricane Katrina my girls convinced me to sell my home and move to Texas, and I don't regret it. I have found this change to be a true blessing from God. I now live in a beautiful home with my daughter Maria, her husband, and their daughter. They are very good to me, and I enjoy them very much.

It is such a relief to not have to worry about the rising property taxes in uptown New Orleans and the high automobile insurance costs. I don't have to worry about plumbers, electricians, renters, house repairs or contractors any more.

When I hear from family and friends, they tell me how blessed I am to have sold my home and relocated to Texas. Getting my Texas driver's license was very difficult, and it took a long time, but I am now a citizen of Texas. I was able to vote for Barack Obama through the mail before getting my Texas license.

My days here in Texas are filled with as much activity as I want. Twice a week I go to the senior citizen center for numerous activities, including socializing, field trips, lunch in town, and dances. I have some special friends at the center, especially the director. They call me when I am away visiting in New Orleans and ask when I will return home. I joined a great Baptist church and participate with the senior programs there. My new pastor is a good preacher of God's Word, and the choir is good too. I still contribute to my New Orleans church as well.

My daughters Joy and Maria always take me places such as plays, movies, concerts, picnics, dances, shopping and other social outings. I am doing so many things that I just didn't do when I lived alone in New Orleans. Only Joyce and Mary and their families now live in New Orleans. I have since met several families who have also relocated to the Dallas area, and we enjoy getting together at each other's homes. All five of my daughters and their families visit me often, and we are all still very close. We had a wonderful first Thanksgiving reunion in Texas in November of 2009. My sister Mattie Bell's son, Johnny

and his wife from Moss Point, Mississippi, surprised us with a visit during the reunion. And, it was wonderful to see them!

A new home! A new church! A new license! New friends! A new life...This is my Story!

www.ingramcontent.com/pod-product-compliance
Lightning Source LLC
Chambersburg PA
CBHW060651150426
42813CB00052B/615